American Moments

ABDO
Daughters

MIRACLE ON ICE

By Alan Pierce

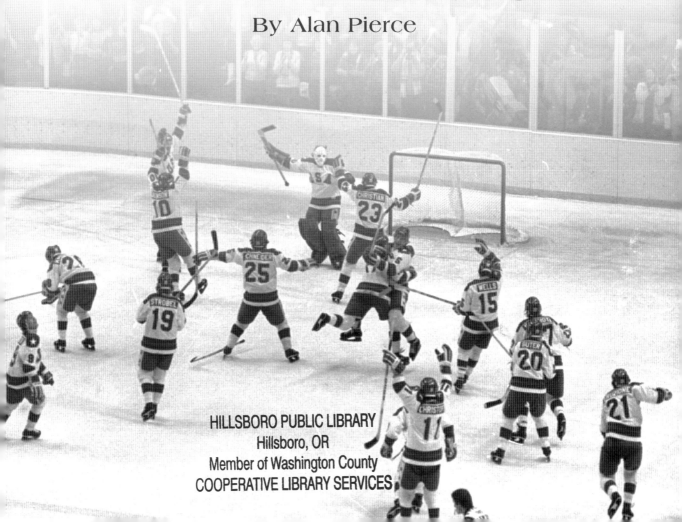

VISIT US AT
WWW.ABDOPUB.COM

Edited by: Melanie A. Howard
Interior Production and Design: Terry Dunham Incorporated
Cover Design: Mighty Media
Photos: APWide World, Corbis, Library of Congress

Library of Congress Cataloging-in-Publication Data

Pierce, Alan, 1966-
    Miracle on ice / Alan Pierce.
        p. cm. -- (American moments)
    Includes index.
    ISBN 1-59197-728-2 3971 0263 2/09
    1. Hockey--United States. 2. Winter Olympic Games (13th : 1980 : Lake Placid, N.Y.)
I. Title. II. Series.

GV848.4.U6P54 2005
796.962'66--dc22
                                                    2004050796

CONTENTS

A MIRACLE

The hockey game was tied 3–3. But this was no ordinary hockey game. The U.S. team was playing the Soviet Union in the 1980 Winter Olympics. Many considered the Soviet National Team the greatest hockey team in the world. On the other hand, the United States had assembled a young team of mostly college players. Almost no one believed the U.S. team had a chance of defeating the powerful Soviets.

Even though the Soviets were expected to win, 10,000 spectators crowded into the Olympic Field House to watch the game. The 1980 Winter Olympics were held in Lake Placid, New York, and the crowd at the game cheered the U.S. team. U.S. hockey fans had plenty to cheer about in the third and final period. American player Mike Eruzione shot the puck past the Soviet goaltender.

The U.S. team now led 4–3 with 10 minutes left to play. In the final minutes, the U.S. team fended off Soviet efforts to score. With only a few seconds left, television announcer Al Michaels exclaimed, "Do you believe in miracles? Yes."

U.S. hockey fans had a reason to believe in miracles. The U.S. hockey team had beaten the Soviet team in one of the biggest upsets in the history of the Olympic Games. Some would say it was the greatest upset in the history of sports.

Celebrations erupted throughout Lake Placid. Fireworks exploded in the sky as people chanted "U.S.A., U.S.A.," and waved American flags.

Excitement about the victory spread throughout the country. In New York City, New York, strangers hugged and sang "God Bless America." In Philadelphia, Pennsylvania, the win was announced at a basketball game. The band started playing the "The Star-Spangled Banner" as thousands of people at the game sang along.

Americans were proud that U.S. players had defeated the Soviet National Team. But there was another reason for the excitement. For many years, there had been little to cheer about in the United States. In fact, war, scandal, and an unsteady economy had disheartened the country.

U.S. hockey player Rob McClanahan attempts to score on Soviet goaltender Vladimir Myshkin.

THE 1960s

The 1960s were troubling times for the United States. Early in the decade, the nation suffered through the tragedy of President John F. Kennedy's assassination. On November 22, 1963, Kennedy was fatally shot while riding in a parade in Dallas, Texas. Authorities accused Lee Harvey Oswald of murdering the president. A Dallas man named Jack Ruby shot Oswald, denying the U.S. public a trial that might have answered questions about the president's assassination.

Another event that made these years so painful was the Vietnam War in Southeast Asia. This war was fought between North Vietnam and South Vietnam. North Vietnam adopted a communist government. The South Vietnamese government opposed communism. In 1954, several countries proposed elections in North and South Vietnam to unify the two Vietnams. When plans for elections fell through, North Vietnam decided to unify the two countries by force.

The conflict in Vietnam turned into a battleground of the Cold War. Communist countries such as the Soviet Union and China armed North Vietnam. The United States opposed the spread of communism. It provided military advisers to the South Vietnamese government.

Opposite page: *Newspaper headlines announce President John F. Kennedy's assassination.*

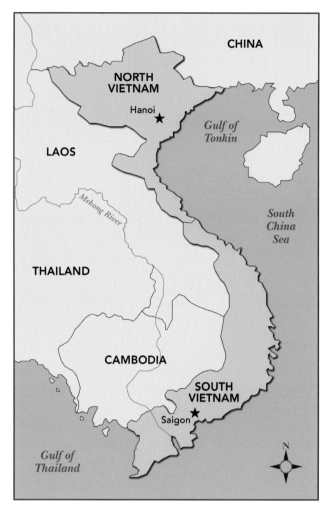

North and South Vietnam and surrounding nations during the Vietnam War

In August 1964, U.S. involvement in the war increased significantly. North Vietnamese patrol boats attacked the U.S. destroyer *Maddox* in the Gulf of Tonkin. U.S. president Lyndon B. Johnson claimed a second attack occurred, but this attack was never proven. The United States then began bombing North Vietnam. The U.S. Congress also passed the Gulf of Tonkin Resolution. Johnson thought this resolution allowed him to take whatever action he thought was necessary to fight the war.

After the resolution, the United States began to commit more soldiers to fight the war. In mid-1965, the United States had about 60,000 troops in Vietnam. By 1967, the number had climbed to 389,000. These forces battled North Vietnamese troops and South Vietnamese communist fighters called the Vietcong.

In early 1968, the North Vietnamese and the Vietcong shocked U.S. and South Vietnamese forces. The communists launched an attack called the Tet Offensive. U.S. and South Vietnamese troops inflicted heavy losses on the communist fighters. However, the Tet

Offensive shook the American public's confidence in the war's progress. U.S. leaders had predicted that the war would end soon. Now it appeared that the North Vietnamese and the Vietcong were still willing to fight.

President Johnson faced opposition within his own Democratic Party because of Vietnam. Antiwar candidate and U.S. Senator Eugene McCarthy had already declared he would oppose Johnson for the Democratic Party's presidential nomination. In March 1968, U.S. Senator Robert F. Kennedy also announced he would challenge Johnson for the nomination. He was the brother of slain president John F. Kennedy. That same month, Johnson announced he would not run for reelection.

Vietnam was not the only place where the United States faced problems. There was also turmoil at home. Some of this conflict sprang from the anger of many African Americans. In the 1960s, African Americans conducted a campaign to win greater civil rights. They made important gains in this area. For example, Congress passed the Civil Rights Act in 1964 and the Voting Rights Act in 1965.

But many African Americans still faced poor living conditions. Unemployment, poverty, and inferior schools were

An American soldier in South Vietnam in 1967

problems for many African Americans. These issues caused African Americans to riot in many U.S. cities such as Los Angeles, California, and Newark, New Jersey.

One man who worked to improve race relations was Martin Luther King Jr. He was known as a great champion for African-American civil rights. His fight against racial injustice won him the Nobel Peace Prize. King also opposed U.S. involvement in the Vietnam War. He called for a cease-fire and for the United States to stop bombing North and South Vietnam.

On April 4, 1968, King was assassinated in Memphis, Tennessee. A man named James Earl Ray shot King, who had been standing on a motel balcony. King's assassination contributed to the disorder in the United States. Riots in more than 100 U.S. cities broke out after King's assassination.

Two months later, the United States experienced the tragedy of another assassination. On June 5, 1968, Robert Kennedy was shot at the Ambassador Hotel in Los Angeles. Kennedy was in Los Angeles to celebrate his victory in the California Democratic presidential primary. A man named Sirhan Bishara Sirhan was found guilty of murdering Senator Kennedy.

Robert Kennedy had been the leading Democratic candidate for the presidential nomination. After his death, Vice President Hubert H. Humphrey became the top Democratic candidate. In August 1968, delegates for the Democratic National Convention met in Chicago, Illinois. They expected to nominate Humphrey to be the Democratic presidential candidate.

The delegates were not the only ones who traveled to Chicago. About 10,000 antiwar protesters came to show Humphrey their

Protesters at the 1968 Democratic National Convention being arrested by police

opposition to the Vietnam War. Chicago mayor Richard J. Daley assigned 12,000 police officers to the streets and brought in the Illinois National Guard for security.

On August 28, a riot broke out as protesters advanced toward the convention. Protesters threw rocks and bottles at police. The police clubbed protesters and used tear gas against them. More than 500 people were arrested and many police officers and protesters were injured in the fighting.

THE 1970s

Humphrey won the Democratic nomination, but he lost the presidential election to the Republican candidate Richard M. Nixon. During the presidential campaign, Nixon hinted that he had a "secret plan" to end the Vietnam War. After he became president, South Vietnamese troops took more responsibility for the fighting.

But Nixon also broadened the war. On April 30, 1970, Nixon announced that U.S. and South Vietnamese forces had invaded Cambodia. The invasion was carried out to attack places where the North Vietnamese thought they would be safe.

The invasion triggered protests on college campuses throughout the United States. These protests turned tragic at Kent State University in Ohio. On May 4, 1970, members of the Ohio National Guard fired on demonstrators, killing four students and wounding nine others. Violence also occurred elsewhere. At Jackson State University in Mississippi, law enforcement officers fired into a dormitory. Two students were killed and nine were wounded.

Richard M. Nixon

William
Schroeder

Allison
Krause

Jeffrey
Miller

Sandra Lee
Scheuer

KENT STATE UNIVERSITY CONTROVERSY

To date, no one knows exactly how the shootings at Kent State occurred. It is not known whether or not a number of guardsmen planned to fire at the protesters. But certain facts are known.

More than 200 students had gathered on the Commons at Kent State University for a peaceful protest at 11:00 AM. They were confronted by more than 70 Ohio National Guardsmen armed with M1 rifles. Protesters were driven back through a football field, over a hill, and into a parking lot. After this push, the guardsmen turned and started back over the hill.

Suddenly, 28 guardsmen turned and fired between 61 and 67 shots at the protesters. The shooting lasted 13 seconds. Pictured above are the four students who were killed. Nine others were injured.

A $675,000 settlement was reached with the victims' families. The 28 guardsmen also signed a formal apology for what had happened. But no one has ever been found responsible for the tragedy.

In 1971, the American people had further reason to distrust the government about the Vietnam War. In that year, the *New York Times* began publishing articles based on what came to be known as the Pentagon Papers. These papers were actually a study of the Vietnam War ordered by former secretary of defense Robert S. McNamara. Daniel Ellsberg had given copies of the secret report to the *New York Times*. He was a former U.S. Department of Defense employee who no longer supported the war.

The study showed that the U.S. government had not always been truthful and prudent about the war. For example, President Johnson approved bombing North Vietnam. However, even some experts doubted that bombing would keep North Vietnam from aiding the Vietcong.

Daniel Ellsberg testifies about the Pentagon Papers.

The Nixon administration tried to prevent the *New York Times* from publishing more articles based on the Pentagon Papers. Nixon was worried that publication of the study would weaken the public's faith in his policy on Vietnam. But on June 30, 1971, the U.S. Supreme Court upheld the newspaper's right to continue publishing the articles.

The Nixon administration was furious with Ellsberg. It had a team investigate Ellsberg. This group broke into the office of Ellsberg's psychiatrist, Dr. Lewis Fielding. The team wanted to find information to use against Ellsberg. But it did not find anything that would embarrass him.

On June 17, 1972, this same group committed another break-in. The group entered the offices of the Democratic National Committee at the Watergate building complex in Washington DC. The intruders were arrested. This burglary started the Watergate scandal.

The reason for the break-in remains unclear. It is also not known who ordered the burglary. However, some of the burglars had connections to Nixon's reelection campaign. In February 1973, the U.S. Senate voted to investigate the matter. During the investigation, the Senate learned that Nixon had taped his conversations in the White House. Investigators wanted to hear these tapes.

Nixon did not want to give up the tapes. His refusal to release the tapes made him unpopular with the public. By late 1973, some members of Congress discussed the possibility of impeaching the president. In April 1974, Nixon released a 1,308-page transcript of the tapes. This action, however, did not stop the process to impeach Nixon.

Nixon received more bad news in July 1974. The U.S. Supreme Court ordered him to hand over the White House tapes to an official prosecuting the Watergate case. Also, the Judiciary Committee in the U.S. House of Representatives made a serious recommendation. It advised that the entire House of Representatives should vote to impeach Nixon. The tapes Nixon released were damaging to the president. They showed that Nixon had ordered a cover-up of the Watergate investigation.

Gerald Ford

Faced with these problems, Nixon announced his resignation from the presidency on August 8, 1974. He became the first U.S. president to resign from office. Nixon's resignation made Vice President Gerald Ford the next U.S. president. Ford pardoned Nixon for any crimes that Nixon might have committed. The pardon made Ford unpopular with the U.S. public. Moreover, the Watergate scandal had the lasting effect of making Americans more suspicious of their leaders.

Less than a year after Nixon's resignation, the United States went through the anguish of losing the Vietnam War. On April 30, 1975, South Vietnam surrendered to North Vietnam. The United States had already withdrawn its forces from the country. But the defeat was still painful. More than 58,000 U.S. military personnel had died, and 303,000 had been wounded.

President Nixon resigns from office.

CRISIS IN CONFIDENCE

The end of the Vietnam War and Watergate did not mean the United States' troubles were over. In the 1970s, the country faced serious economic problems. One severe problem was inflation, meaning the cost of goods and services was increasing. These rising prices created a hardship for U.S. families. Presidents Nixon and Ford tried to control inflation. But these efforts sometimes did not work, or they caused other problems in the economy.

Another problem in the economy was unemployment. In order to fight inflation, President Ford took steps to slow down the economy. However, these actions also caused more people to lose their jobs. In 1976, Ford lost the presidential election to Jimmy Carter. When Carter became president he had to deal with both inflation and unemployment. Carter chose to lower unemployment, but when he did so, inflation went up.

Jimmy Carter

In 1973, a sign outside a gas station in Denver, Colorado, announced that the station had run out of gasoline.

Another situation burdened the United States at this time. The country experienced two energy crises. In 1973, Arab countries that produced oil had refused to sell this energy source to the United States. These nations were angry about U.S. support for Israel in a recent war between Israel and neighboring Arab countries. The price of gasoline, which is made from oil, shot up in the United States. Suddenly, people had to wait in line at gas stations to fill up their vehicles.

This first gasoline shortage ended in March 1974. Arab countries decided to sell oil again to the United States. However, a second gasoline shortage hit the United States in 1979. One Middle Eastern country, Iran, quit selling oil because of political turmoil in that country. Other oil-producing countries raised the price of oil. U.S. motorists again had to wait in line to buy gas.

The energy crisis was not totally unexpected. Utility companies had been building nuclear power plants to furnish an alternative form of energy. But on March 28, 1979, an accident happened at the Three Mile Island nuclear power plant near Harrisburg, Pennsylvania. People were evacuated because of worries about possible exposure to radioactive gases. No one was injured in the accident. However, the incident led people to question the safety of nuclear energy.

The problems facing the country hurt President Carter's popularity. He decided to meet with leaders in politics, religion, and education to ask them for solutions. After these meetings, Carter gave a televised address to the nation on July 15, 1979. The address became known as the "crisis in confidence" speech.

In the speech, Carter listed the tragedies and difficulties that had troubled the United States. "We were sure that ours was a nation of the ballot, not the bullet, until the murders of John Kennedy and Robert Kennedy and Martin Luther King Jr. We were taught that our armies were always invincible and our causes were always just, only to suffer the agony of Vietnam. We respected the presidency as a place of honor until the shock of Watergate.

"We remember when the phrase 'sound as a dollar' was an expression of absolute dependability, until ten years of inflation began to shrink our dollar and our savings. We believed that our nation's resources were limitless until 1973, when we had to face a growing dependence on foreign oil."

Opposite page: *Three Mile Island nuclear power plant*

In the speech, Carter proposed a plan for dealing with the energy crisis. One important goal was to reduce dependence on foreign oil. Another goal called for spending more money to develop other energy sources such as coal, oil shale, and solar power. The president also asked Americans to conserve energy. Carter called any step to save energy "an act of patriotism."

The American people seemed to appreciate Carter's speech at first. But, newspaper editorials accused Carter of blaming the country's problems on the American people. Then Carter fired some of his advisers. This move was intended to show that the president was taking action. The public, however, began to lose confidence in Carter's leadership.

That year, Carter was confronted with another crisis. In Iran, revolutionaries succeeded in overthrowing the country's leader Mohammad Reza Pahlavi, also known as the shah of Iran. These revolutionaries were supporters of Ayatollah Ruhollah Khomeini. He was a religious leader who encouraged the Iranian people to overthrow the shah, who had been a U.S. ally.

In October 1979, the shah entered the United States for cancer treatment. On November 4, Iranian militants seized the U.S. embassy in Tehran, Iran, and took more than 60 Americans hostage. The militants demanded the shah's return to Iran for the release of the hostages. Carter refused the demand. Later that month, the Iranians released 13 women and African-American hostages. However, the Iranians continued to hold 53 hostages.

IRANIAN HOSTAGE CRISIS

Hostages step off the plane in Frankfurt, Germany, after being released.

The Iranian hostage crisis continued to vex Jimmy Carter's presidency. One rescue attempt was staged in April 1980. But it was a disaster. During the mission, three helicopters failed to work. Carter called off the mission. However, a helicopter and airplane collided, killing eight U.S. soldiers.

In July, the Iranians released one hostage with health problems. The other 52 Americans, however, remained hostages. The Carter administration continued to work for their release. Finally, an agreement was reached.

The United States agreed to return $8 billion in frozen Iranian assets in exchange for the hostages' release. After 444 days in captivity, the hostages were freed on January 20, 1981.

COACH BROOKS

During this time of national discouragement, coaches and athletes prepared for the 1980 Winter Olympics in Lake Placid. Among those getting ready for the games was Herb Brooks, head coach of the U.S. Olympic hockey team. He had recently stepped down as head hockey coach at the University of Minnesota to coach the Olympic team.

Brooks had grown up in St. Paul, Minnesota, in a family that loved hockey. He went on to play hockey for St. Paul's John A. Johnson High School. In 1955, Brooks's hockey team won a game in the state playoffs that went into 11 overtimes. After winning that game, the St. Paul Johnson team eventually won the state hockey championship.

Brooks played college hockey at the University of Minnesota. His coach John Mariucci recalled that Brooks was one of the swiftest players in college. Brooks, however, did more than play hockey at the University of Minnesota. He also earned a degree in psychology.

Brooks tried out for the 1960 U.S. Olympic hockey team. He was the final player cut from that team. The U.S. team went on to beat

A statue of Herb Brooks in St. Paul, Minnesota

Czechoslovakia for the gold medal. After the victory, Brooks's father, Herb Sr., commented that the coach had cut the right player. That remark motivated Herb Brooks to make the Olympic hockey teams in 1964 and 1968. Neither of these U.S. teams won an Olympic medal.

In 1972, Brooks became head coach of the University of Minnesota's hockey team. As head coach, Brooks adopted ideas from Soviet hockey coach Anatoli Tarasov. One tactic that Tarasov favored was increased passing of the puck. He believed that more passing improved the attack against an opponent. Tarasov's style also had a big impact on European hockey.

Brooks won three national championships at the university in 1974, 1976, and 1979. After those successes, he was named coach of the U.S. Olympic hockey team. In August 1979, players gathered to try out for the team at a camp in Colorado Springs, Colorado. Brooks would quickly have to cut the number of players from 68 to 26. Eventually, only 20 players would make the team.

Brooks tries out for the 1960 Olympic hockey team.

To help him decide which players to keep, Brooks gave the players a 300-question psychological test. The test was intended to judge how well the players handled pressure.

In addition to having players who could handle stress, Brooks wanted players who were open to new ideas. He did not want players who relied on a physical style of play. Instead, Brooks wanted players who were willing to learn his style of play. This style combined elements of North American and European hockey. It would still be a physical brand like the North American game. But it would also require crisscrossing movements on the ice and more imaginative play.

Determining the final players for the team was a sensitive matter. Players from the East Coast were worried that Brooks favored Midwestern players. Eastern players complained when a fellow Easterner was cut from the team. They were also upset when the band played the University of Minnesota fight song at a team dinner. The team's final composition was made up largely of Midwestern players. Twelve players from Minnesota, two from Wisconsin, two from Michigan, and four from Massachusetts formed the team. Ranging in age from 19 to 25, these players made up one of the youngest hockey teams to play in the Winter Olympics.

Brooks was tough on the young players. He was not friendly toward them, and he worked them hard. Brooks's tough treatment served a purpose. The players became united against him. They worked hard to prove themselves to their coach.

In practice, the players did a workout they called "Herbies." Many hockey teams perform this exercise, but the Olympic players named this strenuous workout after their coach. Herbies called for

Herb Brooks talks to members of the 1980 Olympic team during practice.

players to skate from the goal line to different lines on the rink and then back. One time, Brooks was unhappy with his team's performance in a pre-Olympic game against Norway. Immediately after the game, he made his team line up and do Herbies.

The U.S. hockey team prepared for the Olympics by playing a demanding schedule of more than 60 games in 159 days. Brooks's team played against college and professional teams. The U.S. team traveled to Europe to play teams there. The Americans even beat hockey teams from the Soviet Union. But these victories were not against the Soviet National Team. However, these wins marked the first time the United States had beaten any hockey team from the Soviet Union since 1960.

Brooks held demanding practices and set high expectations for his players because they might face the Soviet National Team in the Olympics. Many experts believed the Soviet Union fielded the best hockey team in the world. The team's conditioning set it apart from other teams. The Soviet Union was famous for having hockey players who were in better shape than anyone else.

But the Soviet National Team also possessed an astounding amount of talent. Vladislav Tretiak played goaltender for the Soviets. He was widely considered one of the best goaltenders to ever play hockey. The Soviet team featured other stars as well. Vyacheslav Fetisov, Alexei Kasatonov, Vladimir Krutov, and Sergei Makarov were considered great players.

Sometimes the Soviet National Team did play against professional players. One case happened in New York City in 1979. The Soviet National Team played a professional team of National Hockey League (NHL) All-Stars in a three-game series. The Soviets won two of the three games, including a 6–0 victory in the third game. Many of these Soviet players who dominated that NHL All-Star team would play in the 1980 Olympics.

Opposite page: *Herb Brooks looks on as the U.S. hockey team plays the Soviets.*

HOCKEY 101

Some basics about the game of hockey

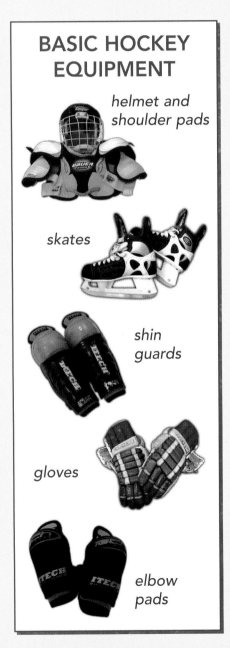

BASIC HOCKEY EQUIPMENT

helmet and shoulder pads

skates

shin guards

gloves

elbow pads

Hockey is played on ice with sticks that traditionally are made of wood, but can now be made of other materials such as graphite, fiberglass, or even titanium. Sticks are generally 50–60 inches (127–152 cm) long with a blade that extends from the bottom at an angle.

Players wear ice skates during the game and use their sticks to handle and pass a rubber puck that is one inch (2.5 cm) thick and three inches (7.6 cm) in diameter. The players try to score points, or goals, by hitting the puck into a net four feet (1.2 m) high and six feet (1.8 m) wide. Each team has a goal on one end of the ice. Team members try to defend their goal while attempting to score on the opposite team's goal.

Most hockey games are divided into three 20-minute periods. During a game, six players per team are allowed on the ice at a time. Usually, one of the six players will be a goaltender, or goalie, two will be defensemen, two will be forwards, and one will be the center.

The goalie's job is to defend the net. He or she wears different padding than the rest of the team. A goalie will usually stay near or directly in front of the net, and will not move very far away from it.

HOCKEY POSITION PLAYERS

Forward   Goalie   Defenseman

The two defensemen are more mobile. They defend the net and try to get the puck away from the opposing team members. Defensemen will also try to prevent or block shots on the net, and they will usually try to get the puck to their team's offense so that their team can score.

Most of the time, a team's scorers are its wings and center. Wings play on the left and right side of the rink, and the center's position is in the middle. Wings assist the center and take direction from him or her. The center and the wings will pass the puck between each other to try to get the puck past the defensemen and the goalie and into the net. At the end of the game, the team that has scored the most goals wins.

HOCKEY RINK

A standard-sized National Hockey League rink is 200 feet (61 m) long and 85 feet (26 m) wide. An Olympic-sized rink is 15 feet (4.6 m) wider. The Olympic rink is wider to allow for more passing during a game.

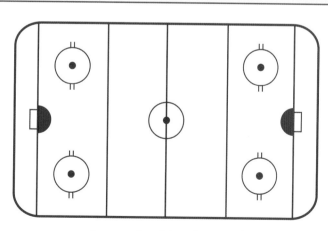

A standard hockey rink

DEFEAT AND RECOVERY

Before the Winter Olympic Games, an international event threatened to keep the Soviets out of the competition. This incident involved Afghanistan. The Afghan government had been friendly toward the Soviet Union. However, other Afghans overthrew this government. On December 24, 1979, the Soviets invaded Afghanistan to install another friendly government.

The invasion increased the Cold War tensions between the Soviet Union and the United States. President Carter thought the attack was a serious threat. He feared the Soviet Union intended to move its forces closer to the oilfields in the Middle East. In response to the invasion, Carter suggested that the United States might boycott the 1980 Summer Olympics. The Summer Games were scheduled to be held in Moscow, the capital of the Soviet Union.

Many assumed the Soviet Union would refuse to participate in the Winter Games being held in the United States. The Soviet Union, however, announced its athletes would compete in the Winter Games. Still, the invasion led to concerns about the safety of the Soviet team in the United States. New York state troopers were assigned to protect the Soviet players and watch for demonstrations aimed at the Soviets.

A few days before the Olympics, the U.S. team played the Soviet National Team. The game took place at Madison Square Garden in

President Carter meets with cabinet members and security officials to discuss the Soviet invasion of Afghanistan.

New York City. As an exhibition game, it would not affect the U.S. hockey team's attempt to win an Olympic gold medal. But it would indicate how well the U.S. team measured up against the Soviets.

As it turned out, the U.S. team failed to play well against them. The U.S. players were dazzled by the Soviets, and even applauded them. In the first period, the Soviets surged ahead 4–0. The U.S. team used a different goaltender in the second period. But the Soviet team continued to dominate the game. When the game ended, the Soviets had thrashed the U.S. team 10–3.

When the 1980 Winter Olympics began, the U.S. hockey team was ranked seventh out of the twelve teams. Some predicted that if the U.S. team played well, it might capture a bronze medal. The U.S. hockey team's style of play might even allow it to upset the Soviet

Union. However, most hockey experts believed that Czechoslovakia and Sweden offered the biggest challenge to the Soviets.

In its first game, the U.S. team played the strong Swedish team. During part of the game, the young U.S. players did not play the style of hockey that Brooks had taught them. Instead, the players relied on the physical style they had been accustomed to playing.

At the end of the first period, Sweden led 1–0. Brooks was angry. In the locker room he yelled at an injured player named Rob McClanahan. McClanahan shouted at Brooks, and some players thought the two might fight. After the frantic intermission, the U.S. team returned to the rink and tied the Swedes 1–1.

In the third period, Sweden took a 2–1 lead. Toward the end of the game, the U.S. pulled goaltender Jim Craig from the net. The move gave the U.S. team another player who could score, but it left the U.S. net undefended. Then, with 27 seconds left, U.S. player Bill Baker knocked in a goal to tie the game 2–2.

The game-tying goal was critical for the U.S. team. To play for medals, the U.S. team needed to win or tie games. Brooks thought his team could only bear one loss.

Next, the U.S. team played a hockey team from Czechoslovakia. Brooks told his players to use their youth and enthusiasm to their advantage. The U.S. players took to the ice and played an outstanding game, routing the Czechs 7–3. With this victory and the tie against Sweden, the United States had played the two best teams in its division. And the United States remained undefeated.

The U.S. team went on to beat Norway 5–1, Romania 7–2, and West Germany 4–2. These victories and the tie with Sweden made the United States one of the top four teams. The U.S. team now would have a chance to play for an Olympic medal. The first opponent in the medal rounds, however, was the magnificent Soviet team.

Before the game with the Soviets, Brooks worked to strengthen his team's confidence. He said the Soviets had lost some of their sharpness. They were ready for a defeat. Brooks also used humor to cut down the Soviet team's imposing reputation. He compared Soviet team captain Boris Mikhailov to comic actor Stan Laurel.

Brooks also reminded his team of their unique situation. The coach told his players that they were destined to be in this game. "You were born to be a player. You were meant to be here. This moment is yours. You were meant to be here at this time."

U.S. player Neil Broten shoots the puck into the glove of Romanian goalie Valerian Netedu.

BEATING THE SOVIETS

On February 22, the U.S. and Soviet hockey teams clashed before 10,000 excited fans at the Olympic Field House. Valery Krotov scored first for the Soviets. U.S. player Buzz Schneider tied the game with a 50-foot (15-m) shot. The Soviets retook the lead when Sergei Makarov fired the puck past U.S. goaltender Jim Craig.

Time was running out in the first period. U.S. player Ken Morrow fired an 80-foot (24-m) shot. The puck deflected off the end boards right to the stick of Mark Johnson, who fired a shot past the Soviet goaltender, Tretiak. The Soviets protested that time had run out and the goal should not be allowed. However, the referees decided the goal counted. At the end of the first period, the game was tied 2–2.

The Soviets made a surprising move at the start of the second period. They replaced Tretiak with a new goaltender, Vladimir Myshkin. Myshkin had played goaltender when the Soviets prevented the NHL All-Stars from scoring.

The Soviets took a 3–2 lead. But in the third period, Myshkin could not stop all U.S. scoring attempts. Johnson rocketed the puck into the Soviet net for his second goal. The score was tied 3–3. About 90 seconds later, U.S. player Mark Pavelich swatted the puck as he was checked into the boards. The puck popped in front of the Soviet net and Mike Eruzione blasted the puck past Myshkin for a 4–3 lead.

Players from the U.S. hockey team celebrate their victory over the Soviet National Team.

In the last 10 minutes, the U.S. team fought off the Soviets, who began to play carelessly at times. Goalie Jim Craig also helped protect the U.S. lead by making great saves. When time expired, the U.S. players threw their sticks into the air and hugged. They were joined by their parents and friends, who rushed onto the ice to embrace the U.S. players.

In the locker room, the celebration was more subdued. The players began to sing "God Bless America," even though they did not know all the words. Brooks thought he was going to cry. He went into the hallway, but the scene outside the hall was no less emotional. New York state troopers were crying.

The emotional response was not the only indication that the U.S. victory was remarkable. President Carter called Brooks to congratulate the team and to invite them to the White House. The U.S. team had made the country proud, Carter said.

CHAMPIONS

Despite the victory over the Soviet hockey team, the United States had not won a medal. To win the gold medal, the U.S. team would have to play Finland. However, there was still a chance the U.S. hockey team might not win any medals if it lost. The players were well aware of this fact. Some players said the team had accomplished too much to ruin their chance for a gold medal.

On February 24, the American and Finnish teams played before 10,000 spectators at the Olympic Field House. The Finnish team scored first and led 2–1 entering into the third period. U.S. player Phil Verchota fired a shot into the Finnish net to tie the score 2–2.

Less than four minutes later the U.S. team captured the lead when Rob McClanahan scored a goal. Mark Johnson added another goal that allowed the United States to take a 4–2 lead. The U.S. team came back to win by scoring three goals in the third period. With this victory, the U.S. team had won the Olympic gold medal in hockey.

The United States victory sparked more celebrating among the players. Many people who watched the game on television were moved emotionally by Jim Craig. While draped in the American flag, Craig looked into the stands and asked for his father. Jim's mother, Peg, had died from cancer two years before the Olympics.

Jim's father, Donald, had praised his son for helping with the family since then.

Hockey spectators were thrilled with the victory. Once again, people poured into the streets of Lake Placid and chanted, "U.S.A., U.S.A." Many people waved flags and sang "God Bless America." Those interviewed by reporters said the gold medal had made them feel patriotic.

Americans throughout the country shared in the celebration. The audience at Radio City Music Hall in New York City sang "The Star-Spangled Banner." The gold medal made Jack Poulsen happy. He was president of the National Fly the Flag Crusade. He drove around Minneapolis, Minnesota, in his station wagon decorated with American flags.

President Carter was also proud of the U.S. hockey team. He called Brooks to congratulate him again. "We were trying to do business and nobody could do it. We were

Jim Craig looks to the crowd while holding the American flag.

39

*U.S. Olympic hockey players celebrate their
gold medal victory at the medal ceremony.*

watching TV with one eye and Iran and the economy with the other," the president said.

Indeed, the gold medal victory helped Americans take their eyes off Iran and the economy. For several years, U.S. citizens had seen a great amount of turmoil and suffering in the nation. But for one miraculous day, they cheered a team that won an amazing victory against the Soviets. And then, they watched this young team capture the Olympic hockey gold medal. It had been a long time since the American people could chant with pride, "U.S.A., U.S.A."

1980 U.S. OLYMPIC TEAM ROSTER

NAME	JERSEY NUMBER	POSITION
Jim Craig	30	Goalie
Steve Janaszak	1	Goalie
Neal Broten	9	Forward
Steve Christoff	11	Forward
Mike Eruzione	21	Forward
John Harrington	28	Forward
Mark Johnson	10	Forward
Rob McClanahan	7	Forward
Mark Pavelich	16	Forward
Buzz Schneider	25	Forward
Dave Silk	8	Forward
Eric Strobel	19	Forward
Phil Verchota	27	Forward
Mark Wells	15	Forward
Bill Baker	6	Defense
Dave Christian	23	Defense
Ken Morrow	3	Defense
Jack O'Callahan	17	Defense
Mike Ramsey	5	Defense
Bob Sutter	20	Defense

TIMELINE

1963 November 22, President John F. Kennedy is assassinated in Dallas, Texas.

1964 In August, the U.S. Congress passes the Gulf of Tonkin Resolution. President Lyndon B. Johnson uses the resolution to expand the U.S. role in the Vietnam War.

1968 In January, the North Vietnamese and Vietcong launch the Tet Offensive. These attacks cause the U.S. public to fear that the Vietnam War will drag on.

On April 4, Martin Luther King Jr. is assassinated in Memphis, Tennessee.

On June 5, U.S. senator Robert Kennedy is assassinated in Los Angeles, California.

In August, police and antiwar protesters clash at the Democratic National Convention in Chicago, Illinois.

1970 On May 4, the Ohio National Guard kills four students during an antiwar protest at Kent State University in Ohio.

1971 The *New York Times* publishes articles based on the Pentagon Papers. These articles showed that U.S. leaders had not always been honest about the Vietnam War.

1973 The United States experiences an energy shortage after some Arab countries refuse to sell oil to the United States.

1974 On August 8, the Watergate scandal forces Richard Nixon to become the first U.S. president to resign from office.

1975 On April 30, South Vietnam surrenders to North Vietnam.

1979 On July 15, President Jimmy Carter delivers the "Crisis in Confidence" speech to the nation. In the speech, Carter addresses the nation's energy and economic problems.

On November 4, Iranian militants seize the U.S. embassy in Tehran, Iran. The militants take American embassy workers hostage, plunging Iran and the United States into an international crisis.

In December, the Soviet Union invades Afghanistan. Controversy over the invasion threatens to keep the Soviet Union out of the 1980 Winter Olympics. The Soviets, however, agree to compete.

1980 On February 13, the Winter Olympic Games begin in Lake Placid, New York.

On February 22, the U.S. hockey team upsets the Soviet Union in a game that came to be known as the "Miracle on Ice."

February 24, the U.S. hockey team defeats Finland to win the Olympic gold medal.

American Moments

FAST FACTS

The Soviet Union won the Olympic gold medal in ice hockey in 1956, 1964, 1968, 1972, 1976, 1984, and 1988.

Brothers Bill and Roger Christian were teammates on the 1960 U.S. Olympic hockey team that won the gold medal. Bill's son, David, played on the 1980 U.S. Olympic hockey team.

In the 1980 Olympics, the U.S. Olympic hockey team came from behind in six out of seven games. Only once did the U.S. team score first. That was the game against Romania.

The success of skater Eric Heiden was another U.S. highlight at the 1980 Winter Olympics. Heiden won five gold medals in the speed-skating events.

Herb Brooks coached two more Olympic hockey teams. In 1998, he coached the French Olympic hockey team, but did not win a medal. Brooks returned to coach the U.S. team in the 2002 Olympics. This time the team won a silver medal.

The end of the Cold War allowed players from the Soviet National Team to play and coach in the National Hockey League. For example, Vladislav Tretiak coached for the Chicago Blackhawks. Also, Vyacheslav Fetisov played for the New Jersey Devils and the Detroit Red Wings.

In 2003, the 1980 U.S. Olympic hockey team was admitted into the U.S. Hockey Hall of Fame in Eveleth, Minnesota. Sadly, Brooks did not live to see his 1980 team receive the honor. On August 11, 2003, Brooks died in a car accident near the Twin Cities in Minnesota.

Herb Brooks also did not live to see the movie released in 2004 about the Miracle on Ice. The movie called *Miracle* focuses on Brooks as he coaches the young group of U.S. players. Actor Kurt Russell portrayed Brooks in the film.

WEB SITES
WWW.ABDOPUB.COM

Would you like to learn more about the Miracle on Ice? Please visit **www.abdopub.com** to find up-to-date Web site links about the Miracle on Ice and other American moments. These links are routinely monitored and updated to provide the most current information available.

The U.S. Olympic hockey team celebrates its victory over Finland in the gold medal game at the 1980 Winter Olympics in Lake Placid, New York.

GLOSSARY

assassinate: to murder a very important person.

asset: something of value. When a government freezes assets, it is stopping the production of the assets.

civil rights: the individual rights of a citizen, such as the right to vote or freedom of speech.

Civil Rights Act: an act passed in 1964 that made discrimination based on race, religion, or national origin unlawful.

Cold War: the mainly diplomatic conflict waged between the United States and the former Soviet Union after World War II. The Cold War resulted in a large buildup of weapons and troops. It ended when the Soviet Union broke up in the late 1980s and early 1990s.

communism: a social and economic system in which everything is owned by the government and given to the people as needed.

Democrat: a member of the Democratic Party. Democrats believe in social change and strong government.

hostage: a person being held against his or her will by a criminal who wants to make a deal with authorities.

House of Representatives: the lower house in the U.S. Congress. Citizens elect members of the house to make laws for the nation.

impeach: to have a trial to see if a person should be removed from office.

Judiciary Committee: a group of legislators in the U.S. House of Representatives that deals with the federal courts and law enforcement. The committee also considers impeachment charges against the president.

psychiatrist: a doctor who treats mental, behavioral, and emotional problems.

psychology: the study of the mind and reasons for the way that people think and act.

Republican: a political party that is conservative and believes in small government.

Senate: the upper house in the U.S. Congress. The Senate has two members from each state in the Union. They make laws for the country.

Tet Offensive: In 1968, North Vietnam launched a surprise attack against American and South Vietnamese forces on the eve of the Vietnamese lunar New Year celebration of Tet. Provincial capitals were seized, military targets attacked, and the U.S. embassy in Saigon was invaded. The offensive was costly to North Vietnam, which suffered heavy casualties. But it was a media disaster for the United States, which could no longer convince the American public that it was in control of the war.

Voting Rights Act: the act from 1965 that removed all barriers meant to keep African Americans from voting. These barriers included literacy tests and poll taxes.

INDEX